PUT YOUR
BEST FOOT FORWARD

RUSSIA

PUT YOUR
BEST FOOT FORWARD

((RUSSIA))

*A Fearless
Guide to
International
Communication
and Behavior*

MARY
MURRAY
BOSROCK

IES
International Education Systems

Library of Congress Publisher's Cataloging-in-Publication Data

Bosrock, Mary Murray.
    Put your best foot forward—Russia: a fearless
guide to international communication and behavior/
Mary Murray Bosrock.
        p. cm.— (Put your best foot forward; bk. 4)
    Includes index.
    Preassigned LCCN: 94-78482
    ISBN 0-9637530-6-1
        1. Russia (Federation)—Guidebooks. 2. Russia
(Federation)—Social life and customs. I. Title. II. Series:
Bosrock, Mary Murray. Put your best foot forward; bk. 4.

DK510.22.B67 1994   914.704'86
                                             QBI94-1733

Printed in the United States of America
10 9 8 7 6 5 4 3 2 1

*In Memory of
my brother Bob and my friend Cathy Faoro—
you left us so young but your shining
example of courage lives on.*

*To Katie Marshall
who fights valiently to live another day—
the same day most of us take for granted.*

Look for other international education
products from IES,
including:

Put Your Best Foot Forward — Asia
Put Your Best Foot Forward — Europe
Put Your Best Foot Forward — Mexico /Canada

Research and Production: Michael Trucano
Illustrations: Craig MacIntosh
Design: Brett Olson

TABLE OF CONTENTS

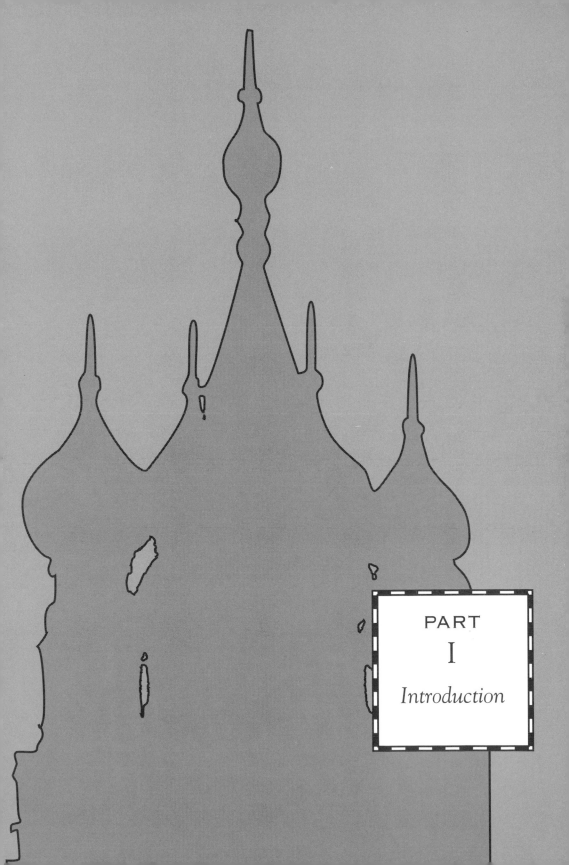

PART

I

Introduction

1.
ACKNOWLEDGMENTS

My thanks to the dozens of people, both
Russian and American—businesspeople,
scholars, diplomats and professionals—who
have drawn on their experiences to contribute
ideas to this book, and particularly to those
who helped review the manuscript.

I would especially like to acknowledge the
following people for all their help:

Dr. Gusel Anulova, Economist, International Monetary
  Fund
Dr. Alexander A. Dynkin, First Deputy Director, Russian
  Academy of Sciences (IMEMO)
Alfredo Maselli
Mary McKelvey
Melor Sturua, Visiting Professor, Hubert H. Humphrey
  Institute of Public Affairs and columnist, *Izvestia*
The staff at the American/Russian Information Resource
  Institute (IRI), Moscow
The staff at the Institute of World Economy and
  International Relations (IMEMO), Russian Academy of
  Sciences, Moscow

Special thanks to Carrie Farrow, Dermot Moore, Sarah E. Seeley, Mark Thompson, Kris Zuzek Volk, and Catherine Walker.

And to all the others who helped and encouraged me in ways large and small, my sincere thanks.

—*Mary Murray Bosrock*
  St. Paul, Minnesota
  Summer, 1994

2.
WHY RUSSIA?

Consider a country twice the size in area of the United States—a country rich in natural resources, forest reserves, enormous energy supplies, mineral deposits, abundant coal deposits, huge reserves of petroleum and natural gas—a leading producer of gold, lead, salt, tin, tungsten, zinc, copper, and silver.

Consider the people of this country, for centuries controlled by totalitarian governments. Imagine their soaring power as the restraints are lifted and the Western world and its opportunities are open to explore. Imagine their energy and enthusiasm as the private sector flourishes.

The Cold War has ended, communism has collapsed—a new era of cooperation challenges both Russia and the United States to forge a unique alliance which will benefit both countries and ultimately the world.

Russia has been referred to as the "ultimate emerging market." However, in order for this promise to be fulfilled, Russia desperately needs

Western investment. Major problems plague Russia's future. The rules of economic life are changing so quickly they are almost impossible to track. The banking system and legal and commercial codes are antiquated or non-existent. Local and national taxes are high and often arbitrary. Rents can be exorbitant and transportation systems are poor. Even theft and racketeering are often a problem.

And yet, while there are many hurdles to overcome as Russia moves from one extreme to another, companies are succeeding and fortunes are being made.

Skyrocketing inflation, high unemployment, and fuel and food shortages make life difficult for the Russian people. Russians, however, are no strangers to hardship. They have survived revolution, civil wars and invasions—all fought on their own soil. 20 million lives, both soldiers and civilians, were lost during World War II alone. Yet despite the ravages of war, famine, and totalitarian dictators, these brave and courageous people produced stunning masterpieces in literature, music, and art. They created a world class ballet, great Olympic athletes, and Nobel prize winners in every field.

Winston Churchill described Russia as "a riddle, wrapped in a mystery inside an enigma." Is Russia really so difficult to understand or is it that few of us have taken the time and made the effort to study and learn about this complex and diverse culture?

Russia is a multi-ethnic country. Each region has its own traditions, language and customs and each is determined to preserve its distinctness. The people are proud of their ethnicity. Even the government recognizes and accepts these differences. This, of course, makes the Russian market difficult to enter and leads to endless possibilities for misunderstandings. Patience and effort are required in order to understand Russia and certainly to establish a business or friendship with the people. However, ask those who have done so and most will tell you the rewards are lifelong and limitless once a relationship is forged.

Look past the images of tanks, parades, Red Square, Lenin, Stalin, the KGB, and communism. Look into the eyes of the Russian people, the people who survived! Their survival alone should earn them great respect. But the Russian people went beyond survival— during their darkest days, they gave the world Tchaikovsky, Tolstoy, the Bolshoi Ballet and the Hermitage.

Will Russia be an easy market to enter? Of course not! You will need a healthy appetite for risk, a great deal of patience and a highly skilled, professional team of experts with excellent contacts and a desire to make a difference.

A peaceful and prosperous Russia means a reliable world partner for trade and prosperity. For those who are willing to enter this market, the rewards could be enormous.

Can Western countries afford to sit this one out?

3.
EUROPEAN RUSSIA/
ASIAN RUSSIA?

Is Russia an Eastern country or a Western country? Scholars have debated this question for years and the debate continues today.

Consider the geography of Russia:

The West Siberian Plain covers 1 million square miles (2.6 million square kilometers). This area is rich in oil and natural gas and is being developed rapidly. Novosibirsk and Omsk lie in this region.

The Central Siberian Plateau is covered with thick pine forests and has a wide variety of rich mineral deposits. Krasnoyarsk and Irkutsh are located in this region.

The East Siberian Uplands are still mainly wilderness covered with mountains and plateaus. This region has valuable mineral resources, but the harsh climate makes tapping these resources difficult. Vladivostok (on the Pacific Ocean) and Khabarovsk (on the Amur River) are the most important cities in this region.

The European Plain is the most densely populated region in the country. Most of Russia's industries are located here, but there are few natural resources. Moscow and St. Petersburg are located in this region.

So Russia extends from the Arctic Ocean south to the Black Sea, and from the Baltic Sea east to the Pacific Ocean, covering much of the continents of Europe and Asia. Russia borders eight European countries, three Asian countries and three countries with lands in both Europe and Asia. Its land is twice that of the United States, covering one seventh of the earth.

More than 6,000 miles and 11 time zones stretch from St. Petersburg in the west to the Bering Straits in the east.

The Ural Mountains form a boundary between European Russia and Asian Russia. While the Russian Far East, with its many resources and business opportunities, certainly would be fascinating to examine, this book has not attempted to deal with Asian Russia.

The vast majority of the population of Russia today lives in the western areas—European Russia. This book is written for the traveler who will visit European Russia, primarily Moscow and St. Petersburg. While this is in no way all of Russia, it is the area in which most visitors will spend at least their initial time.

4.

THE WORLD ACCORDING TO ME

Put Your Best Foot Forward—Russia reflects not only my personal observations and experiences during nearly a decade of working and traveling in Russia as an international businessperson, but also what other people with a great deal of experience in Russia have passed on to me. I'm just "telling it as I see it."

Trying to describe human behavior is tricky at best. No two people behave in exactly the same way; perhaps even more important, no two people interpret others' behavior in the same way. Does this make intercultural communication and understanding impossible for the ordinary business traveler? Certainly not! My own experience in Russia suggests that the only real prerequisite is a willingness to learn.

5.
WHO SHOULD
USE THIS BOOK?

Put Your Best Foot Forward—Russia is intended
to give Western businesspeople the cultural
background and communication skills they
need to interact effectively with Russians—and
to establish the relationships that are the basis
for doing business in Russia. Although it was
designed primarily as a resource for
businesspeople, *Put Your Best Foot
Forward—Russia* should be equally
helpful for leisure travelers, people in the
travel and hospitality industry and
hosts who regularly entertain
Russian visitors.

The information in this book isn't
just "nice to know." It's vital to your
success and that of your company if
you want to do business in Russia or
with Russians. Admittedly, this is a
culturally complex undertaking—but
one that can be richly rewarding for
businesspeople and companies willing to acquire

even the most basic grasp of Russian culture, customs and history.

Knowing something about the culture of your Russian colleagues will allow you to be more sensitive, have more fun and be much more effective in pursuing and realizing your business objectives. It will help you to understand Russians better, and to be understood by Russians more easily.

Keep this book on your desk or tuck it in your suitcase. Before you meet or talk with someone from Russia, you can quickly learn or review important facts that will assist you in communicating clearly.

You will undoubtably still make mistakes, but they will be sensitive mistakes—mistakes made as a result of trying, not out of arrogance. Sensitive imperfection can be endearing. Remember, it's better to make mistakes by trying than not to try at all.

6.

LETTER FROM RUSSIA

Over the past several years, as I've collected material for this book, I've asked a number of Russians how they view Americans and what points they'd like to make to Americans who'll be visiting Russia. The following is a compilation of some of their more interesting comments.

Dear American Friends,

You asked what we Russians think about you Americans. Honestly, we like America and Americans. We admire many things about you. You inspired many of our hopes and dreams of freedom and democracy. From pop music to blue jeans, you have had a major influence on our changing lifestyles. We admire your perennial optimism and can-do attitude, and the way you are able to move about unencumbered by your past.

We admire the society and economy you have created. You are clearly an economic superpower, and when you come here to do business, you generally come with excellent products, competitively priced.

However, you expect to come in, slap us on the back and sign a contract—all in one visit. If you understood a little more about us and our customs, you'd be aware that we want to know you personally before we do business with you. When we do get to know you, we almost always like you.

But as much as we like and admire you and your country, we take pride in being Russian, in the great history and cultural heritage of our country. We feel that the Cold War was fought between two systems—capitalism and communism—and not between the peoples of our great nations. Don't treat us like the vanquished. We are not a conquered nation. Nothing annoys us more than when you act superior to us just because you have more money.

We still like things American, but not every American. We still like you to be our friends, but friendship must go both ways. If you wish to build a relationship with us, you have to learn about what makes us who we are. You often appear to respect only the new and improved, dismissing the venerable and traditional. We rejoice in our great cultural heritage and traditions. We are an old nation with deep roots. Ours is the land of Tolstoy and Pushkin, of Chekov and Dostoyevsky, of

Tchaikovsky and Rachmaninoff. Our customs and beliefs are based on centuries of tradition. Unless you've studied our history in detail, you're in no position to be judgmental.

Get to know us as individuals. While we are a friendly and gregarious people, we must admit that we are often shocked and embarrassed by your openness about your private lives. Respect our differences. We may not have as many VCRs and fancy cars as you do, but that does not give you license to lecture us about equality or morality. We are generous hosts. Please be respectful, interested and appreciative of our hospitality. It is offered in friendship.

Admittedly, we are going through some tough times now. Although many of us are embracing capitalism, the specter of the last seven decades still looms large. Don't expect us to be able to adapt to this new world overnight. But we have overcome adversity before. We have survived tyrants and foreign invasions. We sacrificed over 20 million of our people to defeat fascism in the Second World War, more than all of the other Allied Powers combined. Despite the hardships, however, the strength, resiliency and vitality of our people remain indomitable.

Try our food, enjoy our great music, wander our streets, visit our world-renowned museums, ballet and circus. We are proud of our country,

The strength, resiliency and vitality of the Russian people remain indomitable.

our homes and our traditions, and we hope you enjoy and appreciate them.

Please visit us, but come informed and with an open mind.

Respectfully,

Your Russian Friends

7.
THE TEN COMMANDMENTS OF DOING BUSINESS IN RUSSIA

1. Do your homework! A basic knowledge of Russian culture and history will be richly rewarded.

2. Take your time and be patient. Plan to be in for the long haul. Relationships develop slowly.

3. Be flexible.

4. Hire a reliable team of experts to take you into the Russian market.

5. Always be sincere. It shows. Sincerity is required to build trust. Trust is required to build a relationship.

6. Thoroughly research and know the background of the people or company with whom or which you intend to do business.

7. Ask, look and listen! Russians are very proud of their culture and history and enjoy

teaching others about their ways. A respectful interest will be appreciated.

8. Never act in a condescending or superior manner with your Russian counterparts. There are few things that turn off Russians more than having American businesspeople enter their country, flaunt their wealth and act in a superior and patronizing manner.

9. Likability is the "magic wand." If people like you, they will forgive just about anything you do wrong.

10. Assume the best about people and their actions. When a problem develops, assume miscommunication was the cause. Keep in mind that, as you struggle to communicate with and understand Russians, they may be struggling to communicate with and understand you too. Most people do what seems appropriate to them based on their values, habits and traditions.

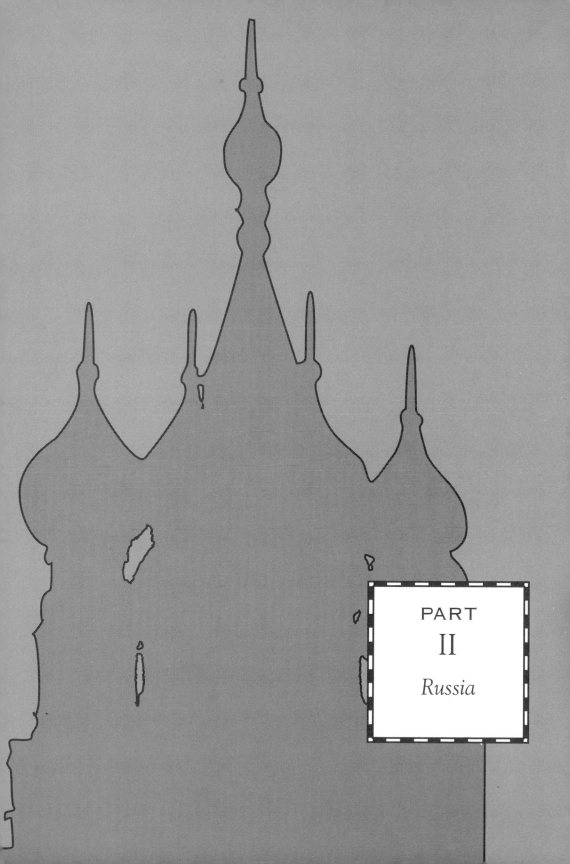

PART
II
Russia

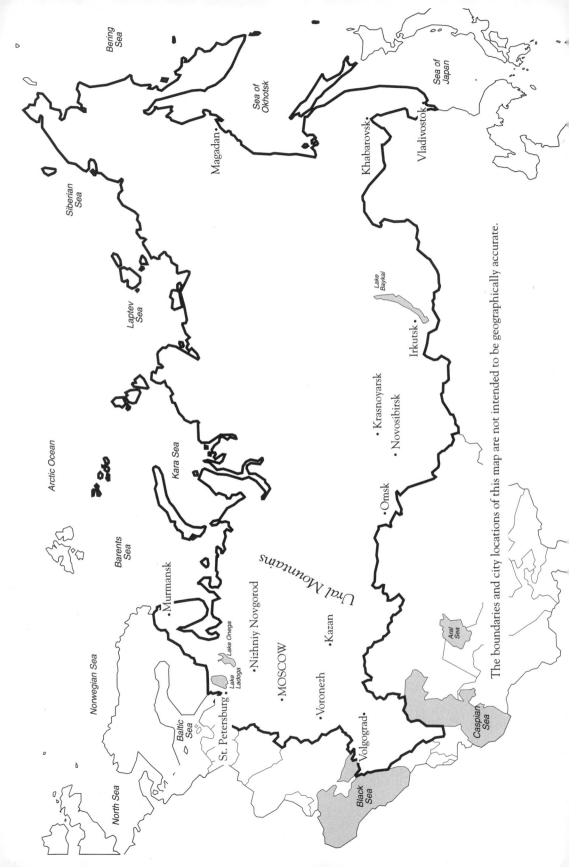

Bering
Sea

Sea of
Okhotsk

Sea of
Japan

Magadan·

Khabarovsk·

Vladivostok·

Siberian
Sea

Laptev
Sea

Lake
Baykal

Irkutsk·

Arctic Ocean

Kara Sea

Krasnoyarsk·

·Novosibirsk

·Omsk

Barents
Sea

Murmansk·

Nizhniy Novgorod

Ural Mountains

The boundaries and city locations of this map are not intended to be geographically accurate.

Norwegian
Sea

Lake Onega

·Kazan

Aral
Sea

·MOSCOW

Lake
Ladoga

St. Petersburg·

·Voronezh

Caspian
Sea

Baltic
Sea

Volgograd·

North Sea

Black
Sea

WHEN YOU'RE DOING BUSINESS IN RUSSIA, ARTHUR ANDERSEN CAN HELP YOU TAKE GREAT STRIDES TOWARD SUCCESS.

Whether it's helping you solve the corporate complexities of doing business in Russia or helping your employees deal with everyday life in a foreign country, Arthur Andersen is ready.

We've been assisting companies establishing or expanding operations in Russia for more than 20 years. We can help you with a myriad of issues such as international tax planning, licensing, foreign tax credits, acquisitions and joint ventures, as well as human resources needs including developing and administering international compensation and benefits policies.

Our experienced professionals in a worldwide network of more than 300 offices in 71 countries share centralized training and a common methodology to assure you high standards and continuity of service across the region and throughout the world.

All of which will help you take giant steps toward reaching your goals.

John Mott, partner in charge
International Tax and Business Advisory Services
212-708-6012

Mac Gajek, partner in charge
International Executive Services
312-507-6810

ARTHUR ANDERSEN

ARTHUR ANDERSEN & CO. SC

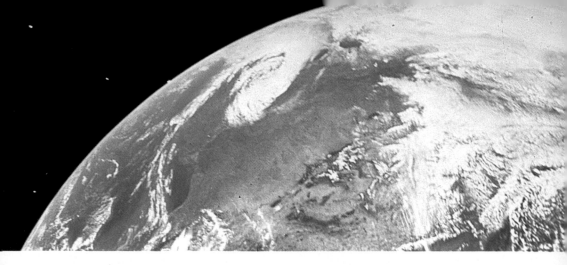

When you take on the world, you're not alone.

You have the security of traveling with the American Express® Card, backed by all the services and people that come with it.

American Express® Travel Services Offices are your home away from home with over 1,700* travel locations in over 120 countries. There you can get a lost or stolen Card replaced usually by the end of the next business day with emergency Card replacement.

With the 24-hour Global Assist Hotline℠ you have a round-the-clock legal and medical referral service in the event of an emergency, when you travel 100 miles or more from home.

So use the American Express Card. You shouldn't have to take on the world by yourself.

Don't Leave Home Without It.®

RUSSIA

VITAL STATISTICS

POPULATION: 150.7 million. 75 percent urban.

CAPITAL: Moscow (population: 9 million). Moscow is the
                    world's third largest city.

MAJOR CITIES: St. Petersburg, Vladivostok, Yekaterinburg
                    (Sverdlovsk), Voronezh, Kazan, Nizhniy
                    Novgorod (Gorki), Novosibirsk, Volgograd
                    (Stalingrad), Irkutsk, Khabarovsk.

LAND SIZE: 17,075,400 square kilometers. Largest country in
                    the world.

GOVERNMENT: The Russian government is in a state of
                    transition. Approved by voters in December,
                    1993, Russia's new constitution consolidates a
                    great deal of power in the office of the presidency.
                    The president functions as head of state,
                    commander-in-chief and head of the security
                    council. The president nominates the prime
                    minister and the deputy prime minister, who

must be approved by the State Duma. If the State Duma rejects the president's nominations twice, the president may dissolve it and call for new elections. The president can declare war and, subject to the approval of the upper house, the president may declare a state of emergency or martial law (although what happens if this approval is not forthcoming is open to interpretation).

Two house parliament. The 178-member upper house, known as the Council of the Federation, has jurisdiction over the army, and between the central government and the provinces. It must approve economic or defense-related legislation passed by the lower house. The 450-member lower house, the State Duma, approves government appointees and fiscal and monetary policy.

Naturally, there are governmental issues and procedures still to be clarified. In time, however, experience and practice will perfect the system.

LIVING STANDARD: GDP = US$6,198 per capita. According to the World Bank, Russian per capita GDP, declining since 1988, is expected to start growing again in 1996.

NATURAL RESOURCES: Coal, iron ore, petroleum, natural gas, manganese, nickel, platinum, lumber.

AGRICULTURE: Wheat, barley, cattle, flax, fruit, hogs, oats, potatoes, rye, sheep, sugar beets, sunflowers.

INDUSTRIES: Oil and gas production, ferrous and nonferrous metallurgy, chemical industry, wood and paper industry, machine building (mainly defense-related). Privatization and military conversion are two major challenges facing the Russian economy.

CLIMATE: Quite varied because of the size of the country, which extends from the Arctic areas in the north to the subtropical zone in the south, and from the Baltic Sea in the West to the Pacific Ocean in the east. Generally, the Russian climate is dry and continental with long, subzero winters and short, temperate summers.

CURRENCY: Russian Ruble (R). Notes are in denominations of 50,000, 10,000, 5,000, 1,000, 500, 200, 100, 25, 10, 5, 3 and 1. In 1990, the highest denomination note was the 100 ruble note. Larger bills have been introduced to cope with the rapid inflation of recent years. The ruble is divided into 100 *kopeks*, but *kopeika* coins are practically nonexistent.

THE PEOPLE

CORRECT
NAME: Russians.

ETHNIC
MAKE-UP: 82 percent Russian, 4 percent Tatar, 3 percent
                         Ukrainian, 1 percent Chuvashi, 1 percent
                         Dagestanian, 1 percent Bashkir, 1 percent
                         Belorussian. 120 different ethnic groups total.

VALUE SYSTEM: Russia has had a long history of totalitarianism,
                         and Russians have employed fatalism as a tool of
                         survival. A desire to work individually and with
                         personal initiative was suppressed by the Czarist
                         and Communist states. With the advent of
                         perestroika ("restructuring"), the
                         Soviet/Communist value system has been
                         scrapped, but the pace of reform has been slow
                         and many are finding it very difficult to adapt to
                         Western values of individualism and profit
                         maximization. Older Russians are generally quite
                         pessimistic and don't have much faith in a better
                         life in the future. Younger urban Russians have
                         adopted a more Western outlook on life.

FAMILY: The family is still important in Russia, but the
                         hardships of everyday life, particularly the severe
                         housing shortage, are causing a high rate of divorce
                         and a very low birth rate. About 50 percent of
                         Russian men and women divorce at least once
                         during their lifetime. In Russia's central regions,
                         the average size of a family is small, with one or

two children. In Russia as a whole, the average family size is 3.2. The mother is the foundation of the family. The number of single mothers is growing, and attitudes toward single mothers are becoming more tolerant.

RELIGION:

The majority of Russians are atheist—a legacy of Communism. However, organized religion—in particular the Russian Orthodox Church—is making a strong comeback in Russia, and the number of religious people is growing. Especially in the south, Islam is gaining in strength.

EDUCATION:

Generally high education level. University level education in a number of disciplines is comparable with the best world standards. The vocational training network is well developed, but many such schools are short of material supplies. Numerous new institutions for retraining are springing up to help meet the needs of the new market economy.

SPORTS:

Soccer, basketball, ice hockey, gymnastics, wrestling, tennis, skiing, weightlifting. Under Communism, participation in athletic activities was strongly encouraged.

IMPORTANT DATES

800's	East Slavs establish the state of Kievan Rus.
988	Slavic people converted to Christianity by Czar Vladimir.
1237-40	Mongols conquer Russia.
1386	Slavs defeat Mongols.
1480	Ivan III breaks Mongol control over Russia.
1547	Ivan IV, "The Terrible," becomes the first Russian czar.
1604-13	Romanov line of czars started when Michael Romanov becomes czar.
1682-1724	Peter I, "The Great," expands Russia's territory.
1703	Peter I founds St. Petersburg and begins building his capital there.
1762-96	Catherine II, "The Great," continues the expansion initiated by Peter I.
1812	Napoleon invades Russia but is forced to retreat.
1861	Alexander II frees the serfs.
1905	Russia defeated by Japan in the Russo-Japanese War. The subsequent revolution forces Nicholas II to establish a parliament.

1914-17	World War I—Russia fights Germany and Austria-Hungary.
1917	The February Revolution overthrows Nicholas II. In the October Revolution Vladimir Ilyich Lenin, head of the Bolshevik Party, leads revolt that brings down interim government and puts Communists in power. On November 8, Lenin becomes ruler of Soviet Russia.
1917-21	Civil war between Lenin's Red Army and the White Army, with Lenin victorious.
1918	Bolsheviks name Moscow the capital of Russia. Russia withdraws from World War I.
1922	The Bolsheviks form the Union of Soviet Socialist Republics, forcibly incorporating Armenia, Azerbaijan, Georgia, Ukraine, and Belarus into the union. Josef Stalin appointed general secretary of the Communist Party.
1924	Lenin dies.
1929	Stalin becomes dictator of the Soviet Union.
1941	Stalin names himself premier of the Soviet Union. He signs a non-aggression pact with Hitler but Hitler invades anyway, bringing Russia into World War II. More than 20 million Soviets die over the course of the war.
1945	U.S.S.R. declares war on Japan. World War II ends in September.
1953	Stalin dies. Nikita S. Khrushchev becomes head of the Communist Party.

1956	Khrushchev begins a program to dishonor Stalin by bitterly criticizing him. Revolts in Poland and Hungary against the communist governments. Khrushchev sends tanks into Hungary.
1958	Khrushchev becomes premier of Soviet Union and starts a policy of detente with the West.
1961	The Berlin Wall built.
1964	Khrushchev meets opposition of hardliners and is overthrown. Leonid I. Brezhnev becomes Communist Party head.
1982	Brezhnev dies.
1985	Mikhail S. Gorbachev becomes head of the Communist Party.
1986	Gorbachev starts perestroika ("restructuring") and attempts to reform the system by introducing glasnost, "openness," and new freedoms.
1989	U.S.S.R. holds its first contested elections for the newly created Congress of Peoples's Deputies. The Berlin wall torn down.
1990	Gorbachev elected by Congress of People's Deputies to the newly created office of president. He receives the Nobel Prize for his contribution to world peace.
1991	Gorbachev and the leaders of 10 republics agree to sign a treaty giving the republics a large amount of self-

government. Boris N. Yeltsin elected to the newly created post of President to the Russian Soviet Federative Socialist Republic (R.S.F.S.R.).

August 19: Conservative Communist Party leaders stage a coup against Gorbachev government. Gorbachev and his family imprisoned in their vacation home.

August 21: Yeltsin leads popular opposition to the coup. Coup collapses.

Gorbachev regains power and the office of President but resigns as leader of the Communist Party.

September: Interim government established to rule until new union treaty and constitution can be written and approved.

December 8: Yeltsin and the presidents of Belarus and Ukraine announce the formation of the Commonwealth of Independent States (C.I.S.).

December 25: Gorbachev resigns as Soviet President. Communist rule ended. Soviet Union ceases to exist.

1992   Russian government slashes military spending and personnel. Government begins issuing certificates that citizens can use to buy shares in state-owned firms. Steps taken to increase private ownership in the country.

1993   President Boris N. Yeltsin dissolves parliament after it blocks his reform policies.

MEETING AND GREETING

- The first impression is powerful! A good first impression creates the expectation of a positive relationship. A bad first impression, on the other hand, can be overcome only with a lot of work over a long period of time—and we often don't get that chance.

- Initial greetings may come across as cool.

- Do not expect friendly smiles.

- A handshake is always appropriate (but not obligatory) when greeting or leaving, regardless of the relationship.

- A man may initiate a handshake with a woman. A woman does not have to offer her hand to a man. Russian men normally don't shake hands with Russian women, but will probably shake hands with Western women because they've heard they should.

- Kissing cheeks (three times) may be appropriate with close friends.

- Offer one of the following greetings and state your name slowly and clearly.

I wish you good health	*Zdravstvuyte*	**ZDRAHVZT voot-tye**

A good first impression creates the expectation of a positive relationship.

| Good day | *Dobriy dyen* | DOE-bree dyen |
| Hello | *Privet* | Pree-VYET |

- When asked "How are you doing?" (*Kak dela?*), a Russian will answer truthfully. If things are not going well, the listener should be prepared for a long answer.

Sergei, a prominent Russian I know, loves to recount the following story about the American sense of "privacy":

PRIVATE:
KEEP OUT

Within five minutes of meeting a potential American client, the American was telling my Russian friend all the sordid details surrounding his recent bitter divorce and his son's stay at an alcohol treatment facility. Not comfortable sharing such intimate information with a total stranger, Sergei did not offer up similar information about himself and his family. Instead, he asked about the American's salary. The American was taken aback: "I'm sorry, but that information is private!"

NAMES AND TITLES

- Russian names have three parts. The given name comes first, followed by the patronymic (the father's given name, followed by a suffix *-evich* or *-ovich*, meaning "son of," or *-evna* or *-ovna*, "daughter of") and then the family name. An *-a* is appended to the end of the family name of a Russian female. A Russian woman normally adopts her husband's family name at marriage.

Examples:

Male name: Stepan Arkadyevich Oblonsky (whose father's name is Arkady Dmitrich Oblonsky).

Female name: Maria Nikolayevna Tolstoya (whose father's name is Nikolai Ivanich Tolstoy).

Female name: Anna Arkadyevna Karenina is the wife of Alexei Alexandrovich Karenin.

- Titles and academic degrees, such as president, director, doctor, etc., are very important, and omitting them is considered very impolite. When in doubt, use a title. If uncertain about the correct title, always use a higher title. Err on the side of formality. Russians should be addressed with their titles until you are invited to use given names.

Titles and academic degrees are very important.

Rule of Thumb

Err on the side of formality.

- If possible, ask for a business card so you can see the correct spelling and correct title. As soon as possible, jot down a phonetic pronunciation of a name.

- Once invited to do so (this normally happens fairly quickly), Russians address one another by using the given name and the patronymic. You will impress Russians if you address them in this manner.

Example:

Stepan Arkadyevich Oblonsky is addressed as Stepan Arkadyevich.

- Titles such as Mr. and Mrs. were not used under the Communists. Many Russians find these titles awkward to use, but the habit is being slowly revived, especially in business circles. Westerners should address their Russian business associates with Mr., Mrs., or Miss/Ms. + their last name. Here are the Russian equivalents:

Mr.   *Gospodin*   gos-PODE-in

Mrs.   *Gospozha*   gos-PO-zhah

- "Madame" is also sometimes used as an informal way to address an adult woman, and is seen as complimentary.

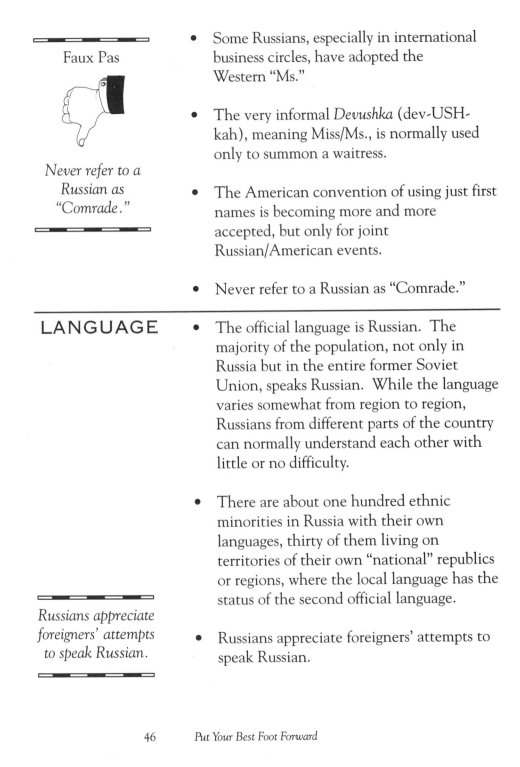

- Some Russians, especially in international business circles, have adopted the Western "Ms."

- The very informal *Devushka* (dev-USH-kah), meaning Miss/Ms., is normally used only to summon a waitress.

- The American convention of using just first names is becoming more and more accepted, but only for joint Russian/American events.

- Never refer to a Russian as "Comrade."

LANGUAGE

- The official language is Russian. The majority of the population, not only in Russia but in the entire former Soviet Union, speaks Russian. While the language varies somewhat from region to region, Russians from different parts of the country can normally understand each other with little or no difficulty.

- There are about one hundred ethnic minorities in Russia with their own languages, thirty of them living on territories of their own "national" republics or regions, where the local language has the status of the second official language.

Russians appreciate foreigners' attempts to speak Russian.

- Russians appreciate foreigners' attempts to speak Russian.

- English is increasingly spoken in Moscow and St. Petersburg by those who have regular dealings with foreigners, and in regional capitals. Because studying English (as well as German and French) in school is mandatory, at least one or two people will speak a little English anywhere you go in Russia.

- When speaking with a Russian in English or through an interpreter, never assume the listener completely understands your meaning; if there's any doubt, repeat what you said in a different way. Use simple, straightforward words—no idioms, jargon or slang (and no sports analogies!). Be aware that many English words have no direct equivalent in Russian and vice versa; many English and Russian words that appear similar may not mean exactly the same thing.

At the height of the Cold War during the 1950s when decisions had to be made quickly, the U.S. ambassador to the Soviet Union was sometimes forced to communicate with the State Department in Washington over non-secure phone lines. Aware that their every word was being monitored and analyzed by KGB eavesdroppers, the ambassador and his counterparts in Washington would speak almost entirely in sports slang. Even though the KGB eavesdroppers could speak fluent English, the Americans reasoned, they had no contact with many American sports. Thus, by the time the Russians could decipher the conversation (if ever), the crisis had passed and secrecy would no longer be so important.

IT'S THIRD AND TEN AND THE CLEAN-UP HITTER IS ON DECK

BODY LANGUAGE

- Russian body language is quite different from American and Canadian body language. Russians are very demonstrative people and public physical contact is common. Hugs, backslapping, kisses on the cheeks, expansive gestures, etc., are common among friends or acquaintances, and between members of the same sex. Members of the same sex may walk hand-in-hand or arm-in-arm in public.

- Russians stand close when talking.

- Do not expect smiles. Russians are generally very serious, especially in business.

- Don't put your thumb through your pointer and middle fingers, or make the "OK" sign—these are very rude gestures in Russia.

- Snapping a finger against your neck indicates that someone has been (or will be) drinking alcohol.

Don't assume your communication problems
are solved once you've hired an interpreter.
In fact, they may just be starting. Some
tips when using an interpreter:

- Discuss with your interpreter in advance
  the subject of the meetings and the main
  points you plan to make.

*Apologize to your
Russian colleagues
for being unable to
speak Russian.*

- Apologize to your Russian colleagues
  for being unable to converse in their
  native tongue.

- Look at and address
  your remarks to your
  Russian
  counterparts, not
  the interpreter. Do
  not place your
  interpreter between
  yourself and your
  Russian colleague.

- Pause frequently to allow
  for interpretation—after
  every verbal "paragraph"
  and, when the subject
  matter is especially important or
  complicated, after
  every sentence.

- Repeat your main points.

- Assume your counterparts can understand English, even if they are using an interpreter; never say anything you don't want others to hear.

- Follow up with a written summary of what was said and agreed upon.

CYRILLIC ALPHABET

Cyrillic	latin	Sounds like	Example	Cyrillic	latin	Sounds like	Example
А	A	*a*	Father	С	S	*s*	sand
Б	B	*b*	bank	Т	T	*t*	tea
В	V	*v*	victor	У	U	*u*	fool
Г	G	*g*	good	Ф	F	*f*	fire
Д	D	*d*	dog	Х	KH	*ch*	loch
Е	E	*ye*	yes	Ц	TS	*ts*	sits
Ж	ZH	*g*	massage	Ч	CH	*ch*	chair
З	Z	*z*	zoo	Ш	SH	*sh*	short
И	I	*ee*	see	Щ	SHCH	*shch*	fresh cheese
К	K	*k*	kind	Ъ	*Hard Sign, Not Pronounced*		
Л	L	*l*	fill	Ь	*Soft Sign, Not Pronounced*		
М	M	*m*	mount	Ы	Y	*i*	ill
Н	N	*n*	north	Э	E	*e*	let
О	O	*o*	port	Ю	YU	*you*	youth
П	P	*p*	pepper	Я	YA	*ya*	yacht
Р	R	*r*	red				

PHRASES

English	Russian	Pronunciation
Good day	*Dobriy dyen*	DOE-bree dyen
Good morning	*Dobroye utro*	DOE-broy-eh OO-troe
Good evening	*Dobriy vecher*	DOE-bree VAY-cher
Please	*Pozhaluysta*	puh-ZHAL-yoosta
Thank you	*Spasiba*	spa-SEE-ba
You're welcome	*Ne za shto*	NAY za shto
Yes	*Da*	dah
No	*Nyet*	nyet
Excuse me	*Izvinite*	iz-vin-EET-eh
Good-bye	*Dosvidanya*	dos-vee-DAHN-ya
How are you?	*Kak dela?*	kahk DEE-lah

MANNERS

GENERAL

- Friendship is highly valued in Russia. Russians depend upon their network of friends to obtain supplies of food, clothing and other items that are scarce.

- In general, Russian manners are casual, especially in smaller communities.

- Do not speak or laugh loudly in public.

- Don't whistle inside a building.

- Remove your gloves before shaking hands. Don't shake hands over a threshold (Russian folk belief holds that this action will lead to an argument).

Russians are great hosts, and love to have guests visit their homes.

- Russians are great hosts, and love to entertain guests in their homes. Russians often put more food on the table than can be eaten to indicate there is an abundance of food (whether there is or not). Guests who leave food on their plates honor their host, meaning they have eaten well.

- An invitation to a Russian *dacha* (country home) is a great honor. Never refuse.

- The traditional way for Russians to greet visitors to their house is to offer them bread and salt; nowadays, this is normally only done at important state functions or in villages.

- Do not turn down offers of food or drink. Given Russian hospitality, this can be difficult, but to decline such offers would be considered extremely rude.

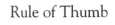

Rule of Thumb

Do not turn down offers of food or drink.

- Shoes are often removed after entering a Russian home, and guests given slippers to wear. Follow your hosts' example, or simply ask them for guidance.

- Russians are very proud of their culture and enjoy the opportunity to talk about their music, art, literature and dance. Knowing art, music and some Russian history will impress.

- Don't compliment an item excessively— Russians may feel obliged to give it to you.

- Don't eat food while walking in the street.

DINING

- Generally speaking, Russians do not have special customs or etiquette for the foods they eat. In more Westernized circles, standard international dining tastes and practices are becoming the norm. Eating is usually continental style, with the fork in the left hand and the knife in the right.

- Except for special occasions like weddings or birthdays, the average Russian rarely dines in a restaurant.

- Never refuse a Russian's offer of food or drink—to do so would normally be considered insulting. If you have dietary restrictions, mention them to your host ahead of time. Russians will understand if you say you have an allergy to a certain food.

- If you have a very weak stomach or really dislike Russian food, here are some tips to help you through dinner: Take a big gulp of the pink stuff (Pepto-Bismol) before you go. Don't chew particularly unpleasant food too much, just swallow fast— sometimes the consistency is worse than the taste. Eat slowly, and engage in conversation with your dinner partners—it will get your mind off the food and take up time until the next course is served. When offered seconds of something you don't like, say "Thank you, but let me be allowed to finish this portion first."

- Many kinds of *zakuski* (appetizers) may be served with a meal. Be prepared for some foods that you may have some trouble with. Cow tongue, for example, is a prized delicacy, and the Russians near you may well watch you eat it. Many Westerners find some types of caviar unappetizing. Following the appetizers will be soup, the main dish and dessert.

- To signal you are finished eating, place your knife and fork side by side (tines up) on your plate at the 5:25 position.

- If you're invited for dinner, don't make other plans for later in the evening. You are expected to loiter.

- At formal functions, guests do not usually start eating until the host has begun. At such functions, no one should leave until the guest of honor has left. If you are the guest of honor, do not stay too late.

Do not start eating until the host has begun.

DRINKING AND TOASTING

- Know your limits when drinking alcohol in Russia! The vast majority of Westerners are unable to keep up with Russians, who consume large quantities of hard alcohol like vodka and cognac. Drinking is often an all-or-nothing affair—moderation is not understood. Saying you don't drink is usually accepted, although Russians may view a man (especially a businessman) who makes this claim with some skepticism. Do your best to play it safe while not offending your hosts.

Know your limits when drinking alcohol in Russia!

- Wine, vodka, port, mineral water or other non-alcoholic beverages are served with most meals. Russians like their champagne and wine pretty sweet. Many Russians prefer local mineral waters because they have a very strong taste.

- Toasts, which are sometimes lengthy and occasionally humorous, are common. The host starts and the guests reply.

- There are no specific rules for toasting in Russia, but generally the host will offer the first toast. Do not drink until the first toast has been offered (you'll have plenty of opportunity soon enough).

- Russians love to make toasts and will toast almost anything. Be prepared to make a toast for every occasion.

- The standard Russian toast is *Na zdorovye* (na zdor-ROVE-yeh), which means "to your health."

- After a toast most Russians like to clink their glasses together. Do not do so if you are drinking something non-alcoholic.

- Never pour wine back-handed. Russians consider this very insulting.

SNACKS

- In many Russian offices, tea or coffee is served with cookies or pastry during the afternoon.

TIPPING

- Tipping is expected in Russia, especially by foreigners. A tip may well be necessary before service is rendered. When in doubt, tip. Russians prefer (and often demand) tips in hard currency.

- Restaurants: Check your bill to see if a service charge is included. If not, leave 10 to 15 percent on the table. If you pay with a credit card, leave your tip in cash on the table—otherwise, your server will not get the tip.

- Taxis: One or two dollars in hard currency is appropriate for taxis. For ruble or "gypsy" taxis, the tip will be included in the total charges.

- Ushers: $1.

- Toilet attendants: Small change.

- Coat check: $1 in good hotels and restaurants.

- Bellmen: $1 in good hotels.

- Hairdressers/Barbers: 10 percent.

- Maids: Small souvenir, small change.

- Guides: $1-2. Guides making hard currency tours are usually prepared to help you with shopping or individual sight-seeing for an extra $10-20.

DRESS

- Russians are tolerant but have an image of how a serious businessperson dresses. Clean-cut is the rule!

Care for clothing is important—shined shoes and pressed cuffs will be noted.

- Most Russians dress in styles similar to those in the West, although they are usually more simple and basic. Care for clothes is important—shined shoes and pressed cuffs will be noted. Western brand names are widely recognized and convey an important status.

- Russian winters are long and cold!! Dress appropriately! Take along warm clothing, including a warm, heavy overcoat, warm footwear, a scarf, gloves and a hat if you plan to be in Russia between October and April.

- Bring a sweater, no matter what time of year you plan to be in Russia.

- Your choice of footwear is important. Russian weather and city grime wreak havoc on even the hardiest of shoes.

- Always take off your hat indoors.

- In winter, the central heating may work too well (particularly at the top levels of multi-level buildings), so dress in layers.

- In the fall and spring, the weather is highly variable, so dress in layers.

- Bring an umbrella if you plan to be in rainy St. Petersburg.

BUSINESS

- Men: Suits and ties; colored, white or striped shirts.

- Women: Suits and dresses, pantsuits. Women may wear high boots in winter.

- A "serious" businessperson is expected to look formal and conservative. Wearing very light or bright colors might make you appear lazy or unreliable to a Russian.

- Ask permission before taking off your suit coat at a business meeting.

Ask permission before taking off your suit coat at a business meeting.

THEATER

- Men: Business attire.

- Women: Business attire, or cocktail dresses on special occasions. Be careful not to overdress.

DINNER

- Men: Dark suits and ties for very formal occasions.

- Women: Cocktail dresses (but don't overdress). A better option is a dressy suit.

CASUAL

- Men: Smart Western casual wear—sweaters, nice shirts and pants.

- Women: Bright-colored dresses or skirts.

- Jeans are acceptable casual wear for both men and women.

- Shorts are tolerated in cities, but are not very appropriate for adults.

GIFTS

- Russians love to give gifts and give them often, especially at special occasions like birthdays, weddings and holidays. Be prepared to reciprocate.

Russians love to give gifts.

- As a general rule, do not give items that, while perhaps a decade ago weren't commonly available (like cigarettes and chewing gum), are now easily obtainable in Russia.

HOSTESS

- An international visitor is an honored guest in a Russian home. Bring a gift for the hostess when visiting a Russian home. Present the gift upon arrival. A small gift for a Russian child is always appropriate (and appreciated).

- Give: Flowers (in odd numbers) and wine. Other good gifts include vodka, candy, a cake, cookies, perfume, books, jeans. What is given is usually less important than the friendship expressed by the act.

- Do not give: An even number of flowers (which are given at funerals).

BUSINESS:

- A small business gift is always appropriate, but its value should correspond to the level of importance of the Russian businessperson with whom you are meeting.

- Present your business gift at the end of a meeting, saying "Here is a small souvenir from our country/company."

- Bring a gift or gifts for the Russian staff in the office. Suggested gifts: Chocolates, coffee, tea, office accessories.

- Give: Decorative plates, pens, pocket calculators, books, music. Gifts with your company logo are appropriate.

- Do not give: Clothes, personal items.

Keep a small supply of knick-knacks from home to give to Russians you meet.

DAILY LIFE

- For other, every-day occasions, keep a small supply of knick-knacks from home, like postcards, pens, pins, buttons, etc. to give to Russians you meet.

DO

- Learn Russian! Learning the language is of incalcuable value, and is the best way to win friends for yourself, your company and your country. If that simply isn't possible, try to learn at least a few phrases in Russian. It doesn't have to be perfect; Russians greatly appreciate any attempt by foreigners to speak their language. Learn the Cyrillic alphabet—your short investment in time will be paid back almost immediately.

- Be alert to street crime. See additional information under Health and Safety for more details.

- Ask for very detailed directions on how to reach your intended destination. Street addresses are often difficult to find on the outside of buildings and normally refer to an entire building or complex (known as a *dom*, or "house" in Russian). Know exactly which entrance you are to use (often there are many).

- Be alert to credit card fraud. One of the common tricks is changing the charged total after you have signed. Check you statements carefully and always keep receipts.

HELPFUL HINTS

Rule of Thumb

*Try to learn at least
a few phrases
in Russian.*

*Ask for very
detailed directions.*

- Take cash with you when traveling in Russia. Many places do not accept credit cards or checks. Cash is usually the best way to pay Russian individuals for services rendered (translators, consultants, etc.). Take along plenty of one dollar bills to be used for tipping.

- When visiting a Russian Orthodox church, women should wear a skirt and preferably have their heads covered. Men should remove their hats. Do not sit with your legs crossed.

- Do feel free to bargain at kiosks (but not in state stores, where the prices are fixed).

- Bring along the following items, which will help make your stay in Russia more comfortable and pleasurable: An alarm clock; aspirin and something to ease stomach discomfort; extra photocopies of your passport, visa, etc.; laundry detergent; an umbrella; extra pens; an extra roll of toilet paper; some snack foods to help keep up your energy levels when events conspire to keep you from eating.

*Service available from over 90 countries. ©MCI Telecommunications Corporation, 1994.

NOW YOU CAN TURN VIRTUALLY ANY PHONE IN THE WORLD INTO A WORLDPHONE.®

All you need to know is the WorldPhone* access number for the country you're in. Dial this access number, and you will get an operator who speaks English, and economical rates from overseas.

Call from country to country, or to the U.S., without intimidation or complications. No language barriers. No currency problems. No outrageous hotel surcharges.

For more information on WorldPhone, call 1-800-996-7535 in the U.S. or call the WorldPhone number from the country you're in.

WORLDPHONE
From MCI

Let It Take You Around The World.

Austria (CC)♦	022-903-012	**Italy** (CC)♦	172-1022	**Switzerland** (CC)♦	155-0222
Belgium (CC)♦	0800-10012	**Luxembourg**	0800-0112	**Turkey** (CC)♦	00-8001-1177
Canada (CC)	1-800-888-8000	**Mexico**▲	95-800-674-7000	**United Kingdom** (CC)	
Denmark (CC)♦	8001-0022	**Netherlands** (CC)♦	06-022-91-22	To call to the U.S.	
Finland (CC)♦	9800-102-80	**Netherlands Antilles** (CC)✛	001-800-	using BT†	0800-89-0222
France (CC)♦	19▼-00-19		950-1022	To call to the U.S.	
Germany (CC)	0130-0012	**Norway** (CC)♦	800-19912	using MERCURY†	0500-89-0222
(Limited availability in eastern Germany.)		**Portugal** (CC)	05-017-1234	To call anywhere other	
Greece (CC)♦	00-800-1211	**Russia** (CC)✛	8▼10-800-497-7222	than the U.S.†	0500-800-800
Ireland (CC)	1-800-55-1001	**Spain** (CC)	900-99-0014		

Use your MCI Card,® local telephone card or call collect...all at the same low rates. (CC) Country-to-country calling available. May not be available to/from all international locations. Certain restrictions apply. ♦ Public phones may require deposit of coin or phone card for dial tone. † International communications carrier. ✛ Limited availability. ▼ Wait for second dial tone. ▲ Available from LADATEL public phones only. All WorldPhone calls are subject to a $2.49 surcharge and per-minute rates.

DO NOT

- Do not discuss personal affairs until a friendship is established. Russians value privacy.

- Do not engage in ostentatious or noisy behavior—such conduct is frowned upon.

- Do not shake hands or kiss across a threshold.

- Do not change money on the black market. The official exchange rate at numerous banks and legal exchange offices is practically the same as on the black market. Thus, there is no need to change on the street, where you will probably be cheated or robbed.

- Do not forget to take a few plastic bags with you when going shopping. They may not be available at the store(s) you visit.

- Do not rely on the river to orient yourself in Moscow, for its numerous twists and turns will most likely throw you off track. Better guides for orientation are the metro system and major traffic arteries, both of which are laid out in concentric circles.

- Do not invite a single woman to sit at the corner of a table—Russian custom holds that she will not get married for seven years.

- Never flirt with a Russian woman in a business setting. However, you should light her cigarette, help her with her coat, pour her drink, etc.—it will be appreciated.

- Do not expect to find smoke-free areas anywhere. A standard joke among foreign businesspeople in Russia is that Russian buildings have two sections: Smoking and Chain-Smoking.

GETTING AROUND

- It is often very difficult to hail a taxi, and Russian cabbies are notoriously crazy drivers. Hail a taxi with your arm straight out, palm down. Doing so while displaying hard currency will greatly increase your odds of getting picked up. Be very careful when riding in so-called "gypsy" (unofficial) cabs (about half of all cabs). Never get into a cab that already has more than one person in it! Many Russians looking to make an extra ruble (or more likely, an extra dollar or deutsche mark) will pick you up and drive you to your destination for a fee.

Payment in dollars or another hard currency is usually demanded of foreigners. Expect to pay more at night and during inclement weather. Negotiate your rate beforehand. If the situation permits, haggle and be prepared to walk away as part of your "negotiations." At the airport, order a car beforehand; otherwise you will (literally and figuratively) be taken for a ride. Have your destination written in Russian to show your driver.

- The metro (subway) is very efficient, crowded and dirt cheap. Russians consider many Moscow stations—beautifully decorated with valuable statues and porcelain—to be works of art. Be prepared for some pushing if you ride the metro between 4-6 p.m. Make sure you study the metro maps beforehand so that you can recognize the name of your stop in Cyrillic.

Don't even consider driving in Russia.

- Cars: *Don't even consider driving in Russia* unless you *really* know what you are doing. If you need to get around by car, hire a driver.

PUNCTUALITY

- Russians appreciate punctuality. Business meetings begin on time. When dining in a restaurant, arrive on time.

Don't be surprised if meetings begin late or are canceled on short notice.

- When being entertained in a Russian's home, try to be punctual, although 15 minutes grace time is usually allowed.

- That said, don't be surprised if meetings begin late, or are canceled on short notice.

- Capitalism is sprouting in Russia and a generation of entrepreneurs is emerging. Business is discussed everywhere.

- While being sensitive to Russian culture and traditions, do not abandon sound business principles in deference to purported cultural differences. Approach the negotiations with the same standards you would elsewhere in the world.

- When properly motivated, the Russians are hard workers and have high work morals. In the past, jobs were secure and motivation was usually low; Westerners viewed many Russian workers as "lazy." This is no longer accurate. Russians generally work a 48-hour work week.

- Under Communism there were no incentives for bureaucrats to perform well or even to be nice to clients; this meant that the usual answer to any question was "No." This practice is still found in Russian society today, but "No" is usually not final. One has to bargain and be persistent to get what he or she wants.

Do not abandon sound business principles in deference to purported cultural differences.

BUSINESS CARDS

- Business cards are handed out liberally in Russia and are always exchanged at a business meeting. The ceremony of presenting and receiving business cards is important—don't treat it lightly.

- Most Russian business cards are printed in Russian (Cyrillic) on one side and English on the other. You should do the same, although it is acceptable for a foreigner to present a card in English only.

Business cards are handed out liberally in Russia.

- Check to make sure your Russian counterpart's business card includes an address and telephone number—sometimes they don't.

CORPORATE CULTURE

Structure: Diametrically opposed cultural influences from the old (Communism, central planning) and the new (market-based capitalism) are tugging at the new Russian state. Just like the structure of the society around it, the structure of Russian business is changing rapidly. Russians are rejecting the central bureaucracy that formerly controlled everything, but it still has an important function, and nothing has emerged to replace it. While many Russians are embracing capitalism, many are still rather distrustful of it.

While many Russians are embracing capitalism, many are still rather distrustful of it.

It is expected that a businessperson will show respect to those in superior positions. Russians are sensitive to age, rank and protocol, so show an appropriate degree of respect when it is called for.

Russian business and government leaders are often dictatorial and authoritarian. Many superiors have difficulty delegating responsibility to subordinates. That said, many of these traits are changing as the old system breaks down.

Meetings: Usually representatives of the Russian company or government body are seated on one side of a table and guests on the other. After introductions, there may be some friendly conversation before discussions begin. The initiator of the meeting will clearly state the purpose of the meeting. Coffee or beverages are almost always served, but this may depend on the budget or facilities of the host institution.

Your company should be represented by a specialized team of experts. Presentations should be thoroughly prepared, detailed, factual and void of "salesmanship." Do not expect a lively reaction after you have made a

Presentations should be thoroughly prepared, detailed, factual and void of "salesmanship."

presentation at a seminar or a conference. If nobody approaches you, it is not a sign that the audience was not impressed.

Russians usually negotiate technical issues very competently, directly and clearly but, being newcomers to capitalism, often do not fully understand Western business practices and objectives. You may have to explain the reasoning behind some of your demands.

Communication: While English is not widely spoken in the Russian business community, more and more Russians are learning English, especially in big cities. Your host can usually easily arrange an English-Russian interpreter, especially in Moscow, St. Petersburg and large industrial centers. If you are meeting outside of these areas, or if you require an interpreter for a language other than English, an interpreter should be found in advance.

A Russian will find it difficult to admit a mistake.

Russian businesspeople may put on airs of preoccupation, or assume a tense posture, hasty walk, sullen look or harsh voice as a way of showing the strains and difficulties they have undergone—this proves their worth to other Russian businesspeople. Small talk is brief. Do not let this deter you from pursuing your goals. Russians will warm up to you if you persevere.

Business and government leaders use a commanding tone with their subordinates and a patronizing tone with partners. A Russian will hesitate to admit a mistake, especially publicly. They will also find it difficult to risk offending someone by making requests or assertions. Joviality and cheerfulness may be interpreted as lightmindedness, and might even be seen as impolite. After a meeting, however, joviality and relaxed interaction go a long way toward developing trust.

Ask your Russian counterparts to explain their negotiation process, so that you have a better understanding of how you might have to adapt your tactics. Profit should be defined as profit for *everyone*; your firm's contribution to Russia should always be stressed.

Trying to do business on the phone in Russia without seeing your prospective business partner is very ineffective. If you are given a home phone number for a Russian business colleague, you may call that person at home. Many Russians use their home phones for business purposes. The Russian telecommunications system is inadequate, but improving quickly. The telex is widely used.

You should take along some business stationery with your letterhead for official correspondence

when you are in Russia. Russian business letters are very formal. Start with "Respected," not "Dear." International correspondence to and from Russia should be addressed in the normal Western way. Inside Russia, envelopes should be addressed in an inverted manner:

COUNTRY
Zip code, City
Street
Name

The return address should follow underneath in the same manner.

BE AWARE

> Personal relationships play a crucial role in Russian business.

• Personal relationships play a crucial role in Russian business. Western firms in Russia should spend a lot of time developing personal relationships. Be yourself—warm and friendly, but initially more formal than you would be at home. Russians place greater trust in partners who have established contacts with the state. Many local government bodies and large companies (especially in the natural resource sector) are practically inaccessible without an established contact, although this is starting to change with the increase of private business. If a Russian businessperson likes you, he or she will share personal experiences, inquire about your political opinions and give advice on business and personal matters. Your best response is to listen, agree and thank him or her for the valuable advice.

- Many Russians are distrustful of outsiders. Russians may view foreign businesspeople as too direct, seeking instant profit. Expressing great worry about repatriating profits can feed on old negative xenophobic stereotypes. Russians trust business partners who are older, respecting the assumed hardships they have been through, their experience and knowledge.

- Business negotiations in Russia are lengthy and will probably test your patience. Plan to be in for the long haul. Make an investment in making and developing relationships, which will pay off in the long run. Repatriating profits should not be your first objective.

Plan to be in for the long haul.

- Russians are quite used to dealing with unanticipated red tape and attempting to navigate the vast governmental bureaucracy. More and more businesspeople, Western and Russian alike, are trying to avoid the state agencies altogether, going directly to privately-owned businesses instead.

- A Russian host will give all possible attention to his or her foreign guest(s), and will feel personally responsible for all the difficulties encountered by that person in Russia.

- Most Russian companies and entrepreneurs have difficulty formulating Western-type business plans and will need guidance and assistance. If a Russian party signs a letter of intent this does not insure serious intentions, but it is a good starting point. Usually no more than 10 percent of letters of intent lead to a contract. If you are dealing with a Russian state-owned enterprise, your business must be pursued every day to get beyond that point. No agreement is final until a contract has been signed. Russians like to finalize deals in Russia.

- Be aware that access to hard currency (and the lifestyle and status it buys in Russia) is the primary motivation for many Russians

No agreement is final until a contract has been signed.

who seek to do business with Westerners. Your access to hard currency can easily cause an imbalance in your relationship with your Russian counterparts. Guard against this imbalance being manipulated.

- Thoroughly research the backgrounds of the people with whom you intend to do business—you will run into many self-styled "experts." Also, beware of businesses operating as fronts for organized crime.

ENTERTAINMENT

- Business entertaining is informal and serves to develop personal relationships. Most Russians prefer to entertain at home because most restaurants are too expensive or of poor quality.

- A Russian who is stiff and formal during business negotiations may be warm, gregarious and hilariously informal at a party. Russians love parties and are very generous and hospitable. They may become very friendly and straightforward and ask many questions.

Thoroughly research the backgrounds of the people with whom you intend to do business.

Business entertaining serves to develop personal relationships.

- Business breakfasts are new to Russians and, although Russian businesspeople rarely initiate such invitations, they willingly accept (especially when invited to a Western hotel or restaurant).

- Lunches and dinners with business partners are common. Spouses are not included at a business lunch. They may be included at a business dinner, but often are not.

- A reservation is highly recommended at any restaurant. To avoid having your table prepared with expensive appetizers before you arrive, ask for a *chisty stol* (pronounced CHEE-stee stohl, or "clean table") when making your reservation. Check on the price (which can vary greatly) and form of payment (i.e. rubles or hard currency) prior to making a reservation. What is written on the menu may not necessarily be available— ask when making reservations. Be aware that many restaurants have loud music and thus are not conducive to business discussions.

APPOINTMENTS

- Normal business hours are Monday - Friday, 9 a.m. to 6 p.m.; most businesses are closed about an hour during the early afternoon (approximately 1 to 2 p.m.) for lunch. The best time to reach a Russian business office is between 9 and 10 a.m. Normal banking hours are 9:30 a.m. to 1 p.m. for state banks, 10 a.m. to 6 p.m. for private banks.

- Schedule an appointment a week or several days in advance, although shorter notice may be acceptable. An appointment with a very high ranking official should be made at least two weeks in advance.

- Reconfirm appointments upon arrival in Russia.

- Avoid the Christmas/New Year season and the first half of May for business appointments.

An appointment with a very high ranking official should be made at least two weeks in advance.

ESPECIALLY FOR WOMEN

An increasing number of Russian women are involved in business.

• Russia is still a very male-dominated society. Men are often thought more capable than women in business and few women are in upper management or positions of power. Equal pay for equal work is not the norm, and many women struggle while bumping their heads against the glass ceiling. That said, an increasing number of Russian women are involved in business, and many are assuming more important roles.

• 90% of Russian women work outside the home. Women are well-represented in scientific and technical fields, construction work, etc. Three quarters of Russia's medical doctors are women. However, women still sweep streets and work as farm laborers. While women are definitely recognized, they are seldom rewarded. Most women work because their husbands' salaries are normally too small to support the families alone. It is fashionable for wives of rich "new Russians" not to work.

• Women are initially regarded with skepticism and may have to prove themselves. Before you visit, have a mutually respected colleague send a letter introducing you. Your business cards should clearly state your title and academic degree. If you establish your position and ability immediately you will encounter far fewer problems.

- Foreign women, especially Americans, should expect some hassles and problems, but are generally accepted in the Russian business community. Foreign businesswomen should always dress conservatively and modestly in a feminine style.

- Be womanly. Allow men to open doors, light cigarettes, etc. Even if you think such customs are antiquated or silly, respect the cultural background of your Russian colleagues.

- Flirting is common between the sexes in business circles, but should not be taken too seriously. Expect cultural misunderstandings to arise from the interaction between genders—try not to be too judgmental.

Expect cultural misunderstandings to arise from the interaction between genders.

- Do not get embarrassed or angry if someone treats you in a sexist manner. It may be difficult, but you're in a foreign country, so learn to roll with the punches. If it is absolutely clear that your Russian associate is unable to work with a woman, consider enlisting a male colleague to join you in that particular deal.

- Foreign businesswomen can use their femininity to their advantage. For fear of not appearing a gentleman, many Russian businessmen may allow foreign businesswomen to get away with some things (requests for meetings, favors, etc.) that foreign businessmen aren't allowed.

- A woman can invite a Russian businessman to lunch and pay the bill, although it might be interpreted by some men as an invitation to flirt.

Russian women can be very aggressive in business.

- Foreign women should be aware that Russian women are not expected to act assertively (and never pay) in social settings. However, Russian women can be very aggressive in business situations.

- Moscow has many good sporting facilities (generally hard currency operations) that are open to women.

- Do not eat alone or with another woman in a restaurant at night. Many Russian men see this as an invitation.

- When taking a taxi, women should always sit in the back seat. Take care when walking on the street late at night. Do not open an apartment or hotel door without asking who is there.

- In Moscow, good contacts for foreign businesswomen can be found at the International Women's Club (tel. 253-2508), the American Women's Organization (tel. 202-7175) and the British Women's Club (tel. 199-6907).

AND WHO
MIGHT YOU BE?

When meeting with Russian professionals, it is always important to establish your credentials and authority as quickly as possible. This is especially true for foreign businesswomen, as I learned the hard way on my first trip to Moscow:

At an important banquet to celebrate a successful round of negotiations, I was seated next to a very prominent Russian man. The number two man of the Russian team, Vladimir acted very distant and ignored me throughout the meal. When it came time to board our flight home the next day, Vladimir was very effusive in his praise of the leader of our delegation. "We welcome your return to Russia anytime," he said. "And," he continued somewhat sarcastically, "you can bring your staffperson (he meant me!), too." At our next meeting, when he found out I was the spouse of the leader of our delegation and vice president of the company that was doing the deal, he was outwardly embarrassed and treated me with an almost exaggerated respect!

HEALTH AND SAFETY

Consult your doctor when planning a trip to Russia.

Travel to Russia isn't advised for the old or infirm. Consult your doctor and/or visit a travel clinic—like those found at many university hospitals and major metropolitan medical centers—when planning a trip to Russia. Russian health care facilities are far below Western standards. Shortages of basic medical supplies, including anesthetics, needles and syringes, common medications and antibiotics are widespread. It is strongly advised that you take out supplementary health insurance for your time in Russia and that you consider purchasing medical evacuation coverage. Immunizations are not required to enter Russia, but diphtheria, tetanus, polio, typhoid and gamma globulin boosters are recommended.

Rule of Thumb

Never drink the tap water in St. Petersburg!!

Never drink the tap water in St. Petersburg!! The *giardia lamblia* parasite, which can cause severe diarrhea, is very prevalent in the city's water supply. As a general rule in Russia, avoid tap water (don't even brush your teeth with it), ice cubes and uncooked fruits and vegetables that can't be peeled. Drink only bottled water that is a recognizable Western brand. Food poisoning is common. View all dairy products as questionable. The food and water in major Western hotels and restaurants are normally fine—ask at the desk.

For the most up-to-date health-related information on travel to Russia, call the Centers for Disease Control Fax Information Service at (404) 332-4565 and order the International Travel Directory, which lists more than three dozen documents and will arrive on your fax machine within 30 minutes. Using the directory, you can order the documents appropriate to your trip.

Virtually nonexistent not too long ago, crime has exploded in Russia during the last five years. Foreigners—unfamiliar with the language and surroundings, usually carrying hard currency and always thought to be rich—make especially inviting targets for criminals. Robbery, pickpocketing and muggings are an increasing problem, especially in major cities.

Take precautions against crime.

Take precautions against crime. Whenever possible, explore Russia in the company of a local resident. If you plan to drink alcohol, make sure at least one member of your party abstains. Never display large amounts of money, and keep your valuables well-concealed. Be especially alert in crowded places. Avoid the black market. Never get into a taxi that has more than one person in it. If you are a vicitim of crime, report it to your embassy and the local police as soon as

Avoid the black market.

possible. Don't jaywalk and beware of umarked hazards when walking on the street.

EMERGENCY NUMBERS

In Moscow and St. Petersburg:

> Fire: 01
> Police: 02
> Ambulance: 03

In Moscow, however, these emergency numbers may be next to impossible to reach; your best bet is to call the emergency number of the American Embassy: 252-2451.

The number for the U.S. Consulate General in St. Petersburg is 274-8235.

January:	New Year's (1-2); Russian Orthodox Christmas (7).
February:	Soviet Army Day (honors all Russian men) (23).
March:	International Women's Day (8).
March/April:	Russian Orthodox Easter.
May:	Labor Day (1); Victory Day (9).
June:	Russian Independence Day (12).
October:	Constitution Day (7).
November:	Anniversary of the Bolshevik Revolution* (7-8).
December:	New Year's Eve (31).

If a holiday falls on a Thursday, then the following two days might be declared holidays also. If a holiday falls on a Saturday or Sunday, Monday will also be a holiday.

*The status of the November 7 holiday remains in limbo.

ADDITIONAL RESOURCES

- Invaluable resources are "The Traveller's Yellow Pages" available for both St. Petersburg ($8.95) and Moscow ($12.95). Available in major Russian hotels, or call (516) 549-0064.

- Intourist (formerly the official and only Soviet tour operator): (212) 757-3884.

- Russian Embassy and Consulates General in the United States:

    Embassy (Washington, DC):
    (202) 939-8709
    Consulate General (New York):
    (212) 348-0926
    Consulate General (San Francisco):
    (415) 202-9800

- American Embassy and Consulates General in Russia:

    Embassy (Moscow):
    [7] (095) 252-2451
    Address: Novinsky Bul'var 19/23

    Consulate General (St. Petersburg):
    [7] (812) 275-1701
    Address: Furshtatskaya Ulitsa 15

    Consulate General (Vladivostok):
    [7] (4232) 268-458
    Address: Ulitsa Mordovtseva 12

INDEX

I'D LIKE TO HEAR FROM YOU!

Do you have a story or anecdote about your international experiences you'd like to share with me? Or maybe you'd like to comment on parts of this book that you find especially true and relevant (or, for that matter, totally false or trivial). I'd like to hear from you! Please write me at:

Mary Murray Bosrock
International Education Systems
Suite 313
26 East Exchange Street
St. Paul, MN   55101
tel. (612) 227-2052
fax. (612) 223-8383

Thanks so much, and always remember to Put Your Best Foot Forward!

—*Mary Murray Bosrock*

---

* If we include your story in any of our future books we will send you a complete set of the *Put Your Best Foot Forward* series.

Products Available from
IES

- *Put Your Best Foot Forward - Asia*

- *Put Your Best Foot Forward - Europe*

- *Put Your Best Foot Forward - Mexico/Canada*

- *Put Your Best Foot Forward - Russia*

TO ORDER:
TEL. (612) 227-2052   FAX. (612) 223-8383

OR MAIL TO:
INTERNATIONAL EDUCATION SYSTEMS
SUITE 313
26 EAST EXCHANGE STREET
SAINT PAUL, MN 55101

Quantity	Title	Price	Total*
_____	Put Your Best Foot Forward - Asia	19.95	_____
_____	Put Your Best Foot Forward - Europe	22.95	_____
_____	Put Your Best Foot Forward - Mexico/Canada	14.95	_____
_____	Put Your Best Foot Forward - Russia	11.95	_____
		Total enclosed	_____

Name and Title _____

Company _____

Address _____

_____

Phone _____   Fax _____

* NOTE : Shipping and Handling not included. Call or fax for shipping charges.
We can ship to your customers worldwide.

NOTES

NOTES

NOTES

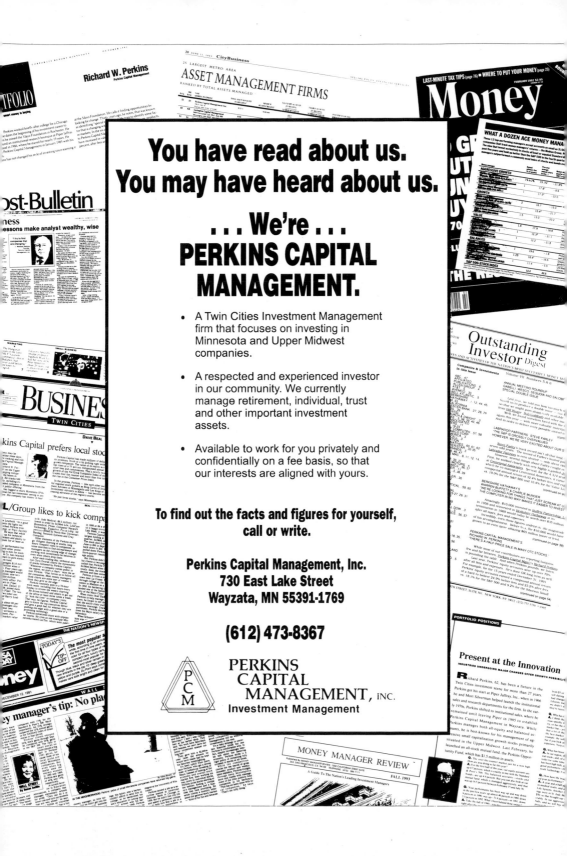

PUT YOUR
BEST FOOT FORWARD

A *perfect company gift for your friends, clients, customers and employees who travel internationally for business or pleasure.*

A Fearless Guide to International Communication and Behavior.

MARY MURRAY BOSROCK

NOTES

NOTES

NOTES

NOTES

NOTES

NOTES

NOTES

NOTES

NOTES

NOTES

NOTES

NOTES

NOTES

NOTES